This page is intentionally left blank.

I0481495

Copyright

Get This As a FREE Audiobook via Amazon's Audible.com

Visit: Bookskim.com/free

The Beginning Of Your Email Campaign:

Where does email marketing begin?

You could argue it begins at the traffic stage of your campaign – and of course, you would be right. But since this is not a traffic report, I'll safely assume you know your market well enough to ONLY target the right kind of people interested in your offer.

After the traffic part comes the squeeze page, yes? So that's where your email marketing begins. It's the "first point of contact" between you, and your visitor – and you know what? First impressions can play a huge part in how your relationship develops.

Too often we hear people talking about building relationships with their subscribers, failing to realize that "before" they become a subscriber, the relationship and trust building process has already begun.

The Traditional "One Page" Squeeze Page:

Almost everyone uses squeeze pages to generate leads. That's how it has always been done – and I'm guessing that's the way you generate leads yourself, right?

But, and here's the big fat juicy "but"

What does your squeeze page look like?

What message does it convey to the person who lands on it?

Do you know?

Have you thought about it before?

If not. Why not?

After all my future email marketing genius. If it's the first point of contact with your subscriber, shouldn't this be a very important thing to know?

Unfortunately, or fortunately from our perspective, most people do not think about their squeeze page at all.

They build out "one page" squeeze pages that look the same as every other squeeze page in their market place.

You know the ones, right? The squeeze pages that "blindly" opt people onto their email lists.

The squeeze pages with nothing more than an image of an eBook/report – and an opt-in form. The one's you are most likely using right this minute to generate leads.

Some have different variations of these traditional squeeze pages, but they still send out the same message to the people who land on them.

They scream ADVERTISEMENT... plain and simple.

The one below demonstrates exactly the kind of pages I'm talking about...

That squeeze page gets an opt-in conversion of 43%, which is very good by average standards. Now, that may be very good for testing your OTO (one time offer) – but the quality of the lead who opts in on a page like this...is very low.

There's simply not enough information for the person entering in their contact details, to know whether the report/freebie is any good.

The report on the above squeeze page is good. In fact, it's an excellent report that I put together. So why on earth didn't I make that fact known "before" the person put their name and email address into my opt-in form?

Well, I didn't know any better back then. I was just doing what everyone else was doing.

I realize now it was a mistake to spend so much time creating a cracking report... only to devalue it by making it seem like just another crappy report you can find on any other squeeze page..

I hope this is making sense to you right now, because it's very important the people opting into your list have a high expectation on what they're going to receive.

The difference between your subscriber having low expectations - and high expectations, is the difference between generating a low quality subscriber – and a high quality subscriber from our first point of contact.

Even when they read the report and it blows them away with the quality. It doesn't mean a thing if they gave me a secondary email address they never use, does it?

And, keep in mind also. If they "did" give me a good email address, but had very low expectations on what they were going to receive... there's a good chance they will never read the report anyway.

I remember reading a very interesting stat some time ago, which stated – *"25% of people who buy information products, don't even open them up to read them."* With this in mind, you have to wonder if people are actually going to read a free report they've downloaded on a crappy squeeze page... that looks similar to any other one they've opted in for in the past.

Considering that if no one is reading your content, you're pissing against the wind. Worth thinking about for sure (not the pissing part – the no reading part)

Some folk don't even bother with an image of their book and a couple of bullet points anymore. They stick up a backdrop image of a beach – and an opt-in form in the centre of the page.

Do they work? Of course they work. But not as well as you'd think. You see, these pages leave the visitor not knowing a thing about the report their about to receive.

There's absolutely NO upfront value or trust given. So what are they thinking before they opt-in? Definitely not thinking you're a marketer who's going to solve their problems that's for sure. Most likely they think… nothing.

They've landed on hundreds of these pages in the past, so this is just another page with an opt-in form and a report up for grabs.

Now let me ask you this…

Do you think it's a good idea to have a person opting into your email list, without them knowing if they're going to get any value from your report?

No, of course it's not a good idea. It's an awful way to generate leads. Because let's face. If someone has low expectations when they put an email into your opt-in form, what are the chances of them giving you a quality email address they consistently use? Little to none, right?

Think about it.

And even if they do give you their primary email address. Do you think these people give a flying monkeys about getting emails from you?

Couple that with the statistics that say 25% never open up a report they paid for... and it's not hard to see that you're wasting precious resources on generating leads that are completely useless, right?

What are your open rates like?

What is the industry standard?

Now ask yourself whether it's a good idea to "blindly" opt people onto your email list.

It's a terrible idea.

Yet everyone is doing it.

And everyone is struggling. Well almost everyone.

I'm no Mystic Meg, but I'm no fool either. If you consistently opt people onto your list, on a squeeze page that gives no upfront value to the visitor... you're asking for trouble.

Why start your email marketing campaign off this way? It's not the smartest approach – and yet everyone is doing it. Why? Simple, they don't know any better. They're thinking of getting "lots" of subscribers instead of "quality" subscribers.

They're following the herd - and they have their heads so far stuck up their own asses they can't see the forest through the trees.

The Alternative "Reverse" Squeeze Page:

What's a reverse squeeze page?

Unlike the traditional "one page" squeeze page, a reverse squeeze page builds trust before anyone enters their contact details into your sign up form.

There's nothing to it, really – but it can start your email marketing campaign off on the right foot.

People are insulated to advertising these days. And like it or not, the widely used "one page" squeeze page with an image and an opt-in form... just screams ADVERTISEMENT!

Not good.

Not good at all.

How do we address this issue effectively?

We focus on giving value before people opt in. We abstain from leading them blindly onto our email list - and we do it all without making our opt-in page look like an advertisement.

If we get this right, we'll have people actually wanting to join our list to get our emails.

Is it difficult to set up?

It's actually easier than the other squeeze page method - and you have the added bonus of standing out from the competition.

We gain instant trust "before" asking for anything in return. Most free reports are rubbish - and most people expect them to be rubbish when they give out their email address, yes? In most cases this is true for sure.

The problem with the traditional squeeze page is that it's a hard sell approach to generating leads. No way around it. But it's time to turn this on its head and gain that initial trust we all seek before our visitor subscribes to our list.

We do this by only asking for an email address after we've given value. This instantly increases the value of our lead, ensures we get a real email address and generates a list of people who want to open our emails. I ask you, who doesn't want to build a list like this?

Let's Get Into The Bones Of The Reverse Squeeze Page

Before we do, I want you to take a look at two examples below of what these pages actually look like...

http://tinylittlebusinesses.com/

http://the-moneymapmethod.com/the-squeeze-report/

You'll notice how...

1) These pages are not like many other squeeze pages...

-- Especially in the MMO (make money online) market where you seriously must consider the consequences of following the herd. People who see the same structured squeeze page over and over again, will automatically place very little value (expectation) on what they're going to receive after they opt- in.

2) These pages build trust by giving value before you see any opt-in form...

-- The one thing that's lacking most in this business is, TRUST (I'm sure you'll agree)

3) There's no BLIND selling (advertising) on these pages - you know what kind of information to expect if you opt-in...

-- Setting expectations from the beginning is HUGE - and almost guarantees you're generating a lead that's highly motivated to read more of your content.

4) There's a link at the end of each page that continues the story (you must click the link to keep reading)

-- If the visitor clicks the link at the bottom of the page, it, a) Ensures they dig your content, and, b) it means they have already taken one action step to get them closer to your offer.

With your every day "run of the mill" squeeze page, you have to create a report (usually at least 15 - 20 pages) but in this case you simply write an 800 - 1000 word quality article and space it out over two pages (much easier)

-- You would put no more than 350 - 450 words on each page (the second page continues the story from the first where there's link at the bottom of the page with a compelling call to action, to make sure they click through.) Make sure to leave a cliff hanger at the end of each page.

-- On the 3rd page you would have your opt-in form telling the reader they must be a subscriber to access the rest of your content (if they clicked through 2 times already this should not be any problem at all - and they'll be happy to do so - after all - you're not forcing anything on them, and you're not leading them down a blind alley)

-- Rather than having an "instant access" button like every other opt-in form has, I'd recommend you have the word "subscribe" instead. This just looks far more trustworthy and it's what almost all blogs use (blogs are far, far more trustworthy than most squeeze pages.

If you still want to use the old method of giving away a free report in exchange for an email address. I suggest you take a look at one of my other reverse squeeze pages here...

http://the-moneymapmethod.com/email-squeeze/

As you can see from the above page, I still give away a free report, but I also created a page that doesn't look like your traditional squeeze page. Not a huge change in delivering upfront value, but even a subtle tweak like this can make all the difference.

What we're after here is people feeling comfortable landing on your squeeze page. We also want them to believe they're getting a good deal in return for their contact details.

Now, don't underestimate the psychological effect these pages have on your visitor. It may not seem like much of a change – but all we're doing is taking them "out" of defence mode – and into "relaxed" mode.

Traditional "one page" squeeze pages do the opposite – and usually result in people putting in fake emails, or secondary email addresses they never use.

Let me ask you this...

Are all your unopened emails the result of people just not giving a damn about your content? Or is it more likely they have given you an email they rarely use? Think about it. Of course, some just won't open up your emails, but to say they are all receiving them... is very short sighted.

Your Homework For This Section Before We Move On:

-- Identify a problem your target audience is struggling with (best to make it a problem they face in the beginning of their online journey.

-- Write an 800 - 1000 word article solving that problem, or at least answering some of the sticking points they will most likely have.

-- Break the article into 2 parts and put it onto your WordPress website (leave a cliff-hanger at the end of each section with a link that sends them to the next page to read the rest of the article)

-- Create a 3rd page with an opt-in form where you tell them they must subscribe to your list to access the rest of your content (opt-in page doesn't have to be super fancy)

That's really all there is to the reverse squeeze page - and should take you no longer than a couple of hours to set up.

Remember, you're zigging when others are zagging - and standing out from your competition will immediately give you an advantage as well as building trust with your reader.

Also remember that the people who subscribe to your list are doing so in order to receive more content from you via email, so no need to worry about fake emails and low percentage open rates. As long as you continue to provide value you'll knock it out of the park.

The Next Step (Your Free Report)

Chances are you will still be giving away free reports on your squeeze pages regardless of what we discussed above. And that's completely fine, I still give away free reports all the time.

But. I still want you to use the reverse squeeze page when doing so. Make sure you give enough "upfront" value – and build that trust before any contact details go into your sign up form.

After they sign up. It's imperative your free report blows them away. Let's face it, most free reports are pretty awful. It's not always the case – but very few people know how to structure a report that motivates their readers to take action.

And like I always say...

"If no one is taking action with your content... they're not going to get results. If they don't get results... they won't value your future advice...period!

Let's put it into perspective. You build a list of 1000 subscribers, okay?

That means 1000 people have read your free report (which is actually the first piece of content they have probably ever read from you – kinda makes it important – obviously all 1000 people are not going to read the report, but you get my point)

In my opinion, 1000 people reading a low quality report is going to have a different outcome to the response of your future email messages, than 1000 people reading a high quality report. Not rocket science, eh?

But I don't see many people paying too much attention to this. Remember, information is just... information. The value it holds has everything to do with how it's presented.

If it's delivered in a lazy manner, it will be perceived in that way too. After all, information is readily available for free all over the place. People skim information unless it's delivered in a way that motivates them to pay more attention. Is this making sense?

That means 1000 people have read your free report (which is actually the first piece of content they have probably ever read from you – kinda makes it important – obviously all 1000 people are not going to read the report, but you get my point)

In my opinion, 1000 people reading a low quality report is going to have a different outcome to the response of your future email messages, than 1000 people reading a high quality report. Not rocket science, eh?

But I don't see many people paying too much attention to this. Remember, information is just... information. The value it holds has everything to do with how it's presented.

If it's delivered in a lazy manner, it will be perceived in that way too. After all, information is readily available for free all over the place. People skim information unless it's delivered in a way that motivates them to pay more attention. Is this making sense?

So, even though you may not think this is an important piece of the email marketing puzzle, it most definitely is. You're in the information business. Information is your main tool you use to get your results.

I think it's safe to assume many, many people in this business over deliver on their promise, and then under deliver with their content.

For now...

I'm going to show you a sure-fire way to create an information product that delivers on its promise.

I recommend you use this template each time you create an information product. If you're not creating your own products, this may be a very good time to start. All that's needed is a 15 - 20 page report that solves "one" specific problem. Unless it's a report similar to this one that needs a lot more information to explain the topic in detail.

How To Structure Your Reports:

Introduction:

Start off your product by telling your reader

- What the product is

- What's the purpose of the product

- Why you created it

- Who it's for

That's what your introduction should cover. A paragraph (4 - 5 lines) for each section will suffice.

Overview:

After you finish your Introduction you then tell them

- What the product is going to cover

- What it will do for them

- Why it's Important they consume the Information

Again, a couple of paragraphs will suffice.

Why they need to learn this:

- What the benefits will be if they know this information

- What they'll be able to achieve knowing this Information

- Why that's a good thing - and how it will change their life

- What they will be able to avoid (slicing the golf ball/freedom from economic control etc)

It's important to paint a picture in your readers mind with this section. Don't assume they will already see the big picture. Conjure up a vivid image.

For example: *If it's a Golf product that helps them hit the ball longer, cleaner and with greater accuracy. Give them an image of standing on the Golf course with their buddies - and seeing the look on their faces as they watch them smash the ball straight down the fairway.*

What it is:

- Give them a summary of what the lesson/technique is.

- Give them examples of it in action.

- Give them the main concept behind what you're teaching.

Why it works:

- Tell them why it works

- What the principals behind the concept are.

- How you found the idea. Who found it.

- Give evidence of it working, either from personal use or from someone else who uses the concept successfully.

How to do it:

- How to implement the strategy/concept.

- What action steps do they need to follow.

This will likely be the most expanded section of your product. Make sure to simplify it as much as possible.

What are the sticking points:

- What are the most common problems they will face when implementing it.

- Is there "one" specific step they should focus their efforts on.

- What else do they need to know in order to scale it up and succeed at it in a big way.

You're winding down the product now after going through the whole strategy previously. This is a very important section. Most people don't take action because they create obstacles in their minds before they even begin taking action. Address these obstacles and they'll be much more inclined to move forward.

What are the emotional outcomes:

- What great things will happen in their life if they take action with it.

- How will their family and partners life be affected if they succeed (if applicable)

- How will they feel once they start seeing results.

- How will they know when they've effectively made it work.

Do not assume your reader already knows the emotional benefits of implementing your strategy.

What happens if they don't use it:

- What will their life be like if they don't implement what you teach.

- How will their life be affected.

- How will their family, partner's life be affected (if applicable)

- How will it make them feel.

Most people just don't take action. So, after you give them the emotional benefits of succeeding with your product, tell them the consequences if they don't take action.

How scalable is it:

- How can they use this strategy/concept in another way.

- How can they adapt the concept to other aspects of their life/work.

- Where else can they use this concept.

If your product can be adapted to other aspects of their life, make sure to tell them what they are. We want to give them every possible reason to take action.

Where to get started first:

- What's the first step they need to make.

- What's the very first thing they need to do once they finish reading/watching.

I'm sure you'll agree that most often it can be difficult to know exactly where to start. This is your product, so you know better than anyone where to begin. Tell them.

Conclusion:

- Paint the bigger picture for them again.

- Give them the motivation to take action

- Conjure up feeling of empowerment.

That's basically the structure of creating an information product that kicks azz. Your product need not be a long drawn out one either. If it's a report for example, you can cover most of these sections in a few short paragraphs for each. Just expand on the most important section, which will obviously be the one that teaches the main strategy.

With our squeeze page sorted and building trust before the opt-in process...

...and our free reported structured in a way that "motivates" our readers to take action...

...it's now time to address "email marketing" itself. In the following sections we will take a closer look at your email messages – and then we'll look at how often we should be contacting our subscribers.

How To Write Email Messages That Get Results:

This is the part that trips a lot of people up. I can understand why it can be difficult knowing what to write, especially with very little solid advice out there relating to this topic.

First things first. You're emails need to be Interesting. They need to engage your subscribers – and they need to have your personality injected into them to help build solid relationships.

With email marketing, we're in the entertainment business. People are bored reading the same nonsense every day when they come online. That's why a lot of them end up wasting their time on social media sites like Flakebook and YouTube.

You MUST separate yourself from the Vanilla marketers already inside your subscribers inbox.

Listen, I read emails from people that I actually know quite well outside of the Internet marketing world. They're Interesting people. Some are funny. Some sarcastic and dry – but "all" have a personality.

But you know what? When I read the emails they're sending to their subscribers. They sound nothing like they do in real life. I mean, they have no bloody personality inside their emails. They're so boring, corporate and Vanilla.

In truth. They are nowhere near as boring in real life as they are inside the email messages they write.

What's going on here?

Simple. They can't seem to express their true personality, because they feel like people don't really care about their true personality.

Nothing could be further from the truth.

Information Is Everywhere

We're not short on information. It's abundant from the blog to the forum – but information is damn near useless if people don't read it.

Information, in and of itself...is nothing but text on a screen. It has no life unless you bring it to life.

Now think about this...

You – and your competition have great information for your subscribers to read, okay? One marketer just shares the information as is. But you deliver the information in a very interesting way that brings it to life, right? Which message do you think your subscribers want to read?

Pretty straight forward, isn't it? When you inject your personality into your email messages... the information you're sharing comes to life. Which means it gets read more often, and also gets used more often too, which is super important.

The difference between no personality inside an email, and having a personality... is the difference between night and day. There's no comparison. And peeps out here are wondering why their open rates are so low. It's obvious this is one of the reasons, yes?

Have you noticed so far everything we've covered is going to help you get higher open rates? While others out there are teaching how to get high open rates by using silly little tricks like writing clever "subject lines," we're

focusing on things that are NOT gimmicks –
and will completely change the structure of
your email marketing.

Gimmicks are fine to add to your arsenal – but
they have nothing to do with relationship
building – and have absolutely no bearing on
the longevity of your email campaigns
increasing in value.

How To Inject Personality Into Your Emails

First thing I recommend is that you dismiss
the notion your subscribers don't want to hear
about your life.

You may falsely believe your subscribers only
want the information – and that's simply not
true at all.

People pay very close attention to others they
can relate to. And believe me pork chop, no
one can relate to information if there's no
personality in it.

People buy on emotion and justify it later with
logic. They must "buy" into your world. Not
with money, but with an emotional stake. The
money will follow.

Information has no emotion. It's how it's presented that makes all the difference. You need to engage people. Create real connections. Keep your communication interesting.

You just need to be yourself. If you have friends, it's probably because you have a personality. That's what needs to come across more than anything.

So, be yourself. Tell stories. Talk about current events/trends. Talk about your journey. The obstacles you've faced, and overcame.

Something, or someone piss you off lately in this business? If there's a lesson to be learned... share it with your list.

Something funny happen to you lately? Is there a lesson that can be learned from it? Share it.

Watch a great movie that got you thinking deeply? Share it. Share the lesson.

See a great question being answered in the forum? Share it. Give your list the question - and then answer it.

A lot of people are talking about "entertaining" in their emails like it's a new thing. It's not. It's called "having a personality" - and not being afraid to share it.

Some people will like it, some won't. I couldn't give a damn about the people who don't. I build deeper relationships with the ones who do.

I will assume you don't knock about with every Tom, Dick and Harriett out there in the world. You have a click of people you can relate to more than others. This, of course... is human nature.

Why then, do people talk about building relationships with their email list – and then write like they're talking to the whole world? I'll tell you something now fruitcake, if you're not being yourself, you're not going to build solid relationships.

Would you rather have 100 people like your content, or 10 people who love your content? I know which one I'd want. Truth is, if you try to appeal to everyone, you end up appealing to no one. I call this "spineless" marketing.

In the beginning it may feel a little uncomfortable to open up and be yourself. It can be daunting for some peeps to open up and truly be themselves. This is natural.

Most often we will only open up to people we know, like and trust, right? And that's what I want you to think about here. If you open up to your subscribers...

...they will feel a sense of connection with you – and therefore feel more comfortable reciprocating. That's when you start getting personal emails from your subscribers... and start building real life, solid relationships based on trust.

Nobody feels comfortable purchasing products from people they don't know. Why would they? This is why top copywriters are in such high demand.

They have an ability to hit emotional hot buttons and get potential customers to drop their guard just long enough to make a purchase.

But you know what? You wouldn't need a copywriter to help you sell a product to your friends. Would you? Your recommendation is all that's needed. That's where we need to get to. If people relate to your story, your personality... they are much more likely to buy from you. Common sense really.

Right. We've established that your emails need personality. It's all fine and dandy knowing we need our emails to be interesting, but it still doesn't address the issue of "what do I write about?"

I'm going to give you 3 templates that you can use over and over again to base your emails around. Once you get the hang of these 3, you will have no problem adding your own templates as you move forwards.

Templates For Your Email Messages

The "Questions & Answers" Email

Pretty self-explanatory, right? You go onto forums, social media, blogs and wherever your target audience hang out.

Look for questions people are asking. Find the best answer, put it into your own words – and send it to your email list. Nothing could be simpler.

Chances are that if others are struggling with a certain aspect of their marketing, and they post a question for clarification... you're email subscribers will probably want an answer to it too.

You've just got a perfect topic to write about, with the added benefit of helping people with a common problem others are obviously struggling with.

What I really like about this template, is that you can make it into a regular thing. Pick one day a week to answer questions in your market – and post them as an email update.

So, Monday could be the day you just send out the questions and answers email to your list. It's a powerful strategy for 2 reasons...

1) You're not struggling to come up with an idea for a message. You're now focused on "one" specific outcome, which is to go find a popular question – and answer it. How easy is that?
2) You're cementing your position as a marketer who has answers to common

1) problems. You see how that works? If you're the person answering the question, then you're the problem solver in the eyes of your list. Brilliant!!

A cool way to approach this is to tell your subscribers that you're answering questions from...well...your subscribers. Start off your email with...

Hi Declan,

As you know, I get a lot of questions from my trusty subscribers looking for clarification on problems they're facing.

Today's question comes from Mark, who asks...

...and then you just segue into the question – and then obviously answer it. You can then tell your subscriber to participate by sending their own questions to you for answering. It's a great way to build trust and credibility – and at the same time... getting your email subscribers to contact you.

The "TV & Movie" Email

Okay, the title is pretty lame, but I'm sure you see what's coming. Popular TV shows and movies that are hot right now are great talking points.

The reason why this email is a good one... is because people are already aware of what's popular right now. So, in essence you're entering into a topic that's already fresh in their minds.

It doesn't have to be something current either. Is there a movie that has inspired you in the past? If so, what in particular about that movie inspired you? There's obviously a lesson in there you can share with your subscribers.

Look at it this way. If you saw an amazing movie, or read an inspiring book, would you share that knowledge with your friends?

You would, right? So why wouldn't you share it with your email list? They're your friends, aren't they? At least that's your end goal... to become friends. To treat them like friends. To communicate with them like they are your friends.

How can you take a popular movie, TV show and/or book and create an email out of it?

Let's look at an example here...

Hi Michael,

You've seen "The Wizard of Oz,"

One of the greatest movies of all time...

The big theme was that the main characters all thought that they didn't have what it takes to get what they wanted in life...

The Scarecrow thought he needed a brain...

The Tin Man thought he didn't have a heart...

The Cowardly Lion was a scaredy-cat...

Dorothy felt lost and wanted to go home...

And it turned out they all already had everything they needed...

But they were looking around outside of themselves, while they should have been looking inside...

You could easily segue that message into anything really. A motivational message. A product promotion… anything. It just takes a little creativity.

But the power in this is immense. You're getting people to think about a movie that quite possibly they have fond memories of. This is important because it creates a strong emotional connection to information that may be somewhat boring and unemotional otherwise. Makes sense, right?

The "Personal Development" Email

This is a favourite of mine. In this business, maybe above any other business… motivation is something every single person needs from time to time. You can easily pick "one" day a week to only send out motivational emails.

Now, I'm not talking airy fairy "fluff filled" law of attraction type nonsense here. Proper advice that ties directly into the problems so many of us face on a day to day basis in the Internet marketing world.

The 80/20 rule is something I write regularly about. Parkinson's Law is another email topic I return to regularly.

Peeps love this stuff in moderation. So once a week is perfect. To give you an idea of something that's so simple to do, but also different enough to help you build solid relationships...

I simply go over to YouTube. Find a 5 minute motivational video. Strip out the audio. Upload it to my hosting – and then share it with my list.

Think about this for one moment....

You find a cracking video that inspires or motivates you. Rather than doing what any other person would do, which is to send a link to the video to their email list (rubbish) you actually went through the trouble of stripping the audio out and delivering it in a much better format that can be listened to on an mp3 player or in the car. Better than just sending a link to a video, right?

Now, imagine your subscriber puts that audio onto their mp3 player and they go for a walk. They dig the audio and it... well... inspires or motivates them, okay?

Do you think they will feel, even somewhat of a real connection with you after that? Maybe.

But one things for sure, it can only have a positive impact on how they perceive you next time you send an email message.

So, my future email marketing genius. Those are just a few templates that you can work off. Nothing ground-breaking, but definitely makes it a little easier if you're struggling with what to write to your email list, yes?

You sit down and create endless templates yourself – and start using them for your emails. A little creativity can make a huge difference, plus, working off templates helps streamline your message writing - and helps keep you focused and on topic. Very powerful in its simplicity.

Let's crack on with the last section of this report...

How often To Email Your List

The Pareto Principle (80/20 rule) is a principle that's alive and well in every single one of our businesses.

20% of customers generate 80% of profits

20% of entrepreneurs generate 80% of new business created

20% of Authors sell 80% of books

20% of your "to-do-list" will be responsible for 80% of your results

And so on...

If we go to any forum and ask the members how often we should email our list, 90% will tell you to email 3 times a week. It's regurgitated nonsense that sits well in the minds of Vanilla marketers who are afraid to test different methods. In my accurate opinion, 90% of marketers you ask this question to... will be 100% wrong.

3 times a week is the sweet spot, or so many will have you believe. The real question is... Is it the sweet spot because it works? Or because it's safe?

I think the reason so many follow this advice is because it's the safe thing to do. Safe, in email marketing is gonna land you in "sametown."

Same crappy open rates as the industry standard. Same responsive rate as your competition.

Same sales to message ratio (if you're good) as the rest.

Safe...is the absolute worst place you want to be when your goal is to stand out.

So, how often should you email your list?

You should be sending an email to your list every single day. I get a great response from the "email lemmings" when I say this inside forums.

Chances are you're disagreeing with me right now. After all, if you email your list every day, they will get pissed off and unsubscribe from you're email list, right? At least that's the nonsense spewing from the majority of email lemmings every time I bring it up.

Do people hate daily emails?

How is that possible? If they really didn't want daily emails, they should just stop signing up to email lists. This will surely solve the problem. Truth is, we all get daily emails. Go to your inbox right now and tell me what you see. Chances are you're going to see emails, right?

So emails aren't the problem. We get them every day regardless. It makes no difference whether the emails are sent from different marketers.

Actually, I would argue that a daily email from one marketer who knows what they're talking about, is a lot better than 20 emails, from 20 different marketers, giving out 20 different marketing messages... that end up pulling you in 20 different directions.

You see my future email marketing genius. It's not that peeps have a problem getting emails every day from the same marketer. They just don't want the same marketer sending the same crappy content to them every day.

Personally, I don't want rubbish content every day ether. No one does. But that doesn't mean your subscribers don't want daily emails. It's a cop-out to say otherwise.

The ones who "really" don't want daily emails, are most likely the same people who have "ADHD" – and who are addicted to signing up to email lists to get freebies. You can make your own conclusion if you want... but these are the people I have absolutely no interest connecting with.

Look at this way: Do you come online every day to avoid learning about your market? Nope. You want to learn new stuff, right? We all do. That's part and parcel of marketing evolution. We educate ourselves. So if you always have something interesting to share with your email list – and your emails are entertaining, do you honestly believe your subscribers will have a problem with that?

They won't.

They don't – and the opposite is actually true.

You become the constant inside your subscribers inbox when everyone else is just dropping in from time to time.

Imagine saying to your partner *"oh sorry dear, I just want to talk to you 3 times a week, it's pissing me off seeing your mug every day"* - Smack in the mouth is what you'll get. If your partner is a pain in the butt, you'll end the relationship soon enough anyway.

If your subscriber thinks you're a pain in the butt, they'll unsubscribe... let them, they're not people you are ever going to build a strong relationship with anyway. We can't... and shouldn't try to be people pleasers. No one likes a people pleaser... even people with no friends ☺

My point here,... is that if you actually like your partner, or close friend, you'll have absolutely no problem hearing from them every day. And this is only a 5 minute email message they have to read anyway. You're not asking them over for dinner and ice cream.

That may seem a wee bit dramatic – and it is, but think about it. Who will build the quicker relationships with their subscribers, the marketer who's just there from time to time, or the marketer who shows up every day come hell or high water? The answer is obvious, providing you're writing interesting and engaging emails.

The more you're there. The more comfortable your subscribers will be with you. This is human nature. Don't believe me? It's true. Take your bad habits for example. You have bad habits, right? But why do you participate in the process of keeping them in your life? It's "familiarity" my genius friend. We become accustomed to whatever we participate in for a sustained period of time. Whether it's good or bad... is not the point.

The more we see something, do something and participate in something... it becomes normal, even if it isn't. That's the power of repetition.

Let me do this another way. I'll give you a couple good, solid reason why you absolutely MUST email your list every day – and then you go make a decision whether or not to do it...

You Become A Better Email Marketer

Writing emails every day makes you a better email marketer. Who doesn't' want this? Think about it. The more you write... the better you get. Who will be a better email message writer. The person who emails 12 times a month, or the one emailing 30 times a month? The answer is blindly obvious.

Not only do you get much, much more comfortable writing emails, but you also have a wider scope of materials to work off. Writing

daily emails is not easy. It takes discipline.
You will, however, become adept at
researching and coming up with new ways and
ideas to get your message across.

This widens your circle of comfort and forces
you to focus more on the

"one" part of your business that you should be
giving "at least" 80% of your time to anyway.

Less Spam Complaints, Higher Open Rates

Bet you didn't see that one coming. If you
listen to most people who fear sending daily
emails, they will tell you that peeps will
complain if you send them emails daily. The
opposite is true.

People complain when they forget who's lists
they sign up to. Have you ever gotten an email
from a marketer and had no recollection of
signing up to their email list? Yeah, me too,
along with the many others out there too.

But that's not possible if you're there every
day. Peeps are not going to forget who you are,
because you're the "one" person they
remember when other email marketers just

pop in now and then... and it's usually just to make a sale..

People also complain when they receive rubbish content from marketers, but we've already discussed this. You are not going to send rubbish. Your goal is to build solid relationships with email messages that entertain, engage – and wrap everything up in a nice little story that's easy to consume and relate to.

You Become A Welcome Guest

We are creatures of comfort. Even our bad habits become familiar to us - and therefore are hard to break. While other marketers breeze in and out from time to time inside your subscribers inbox, you become the constant. Your name becomes familiar to them. They expect your emails – and when they don't arrive, they will feel like there's something missing.

If you're sending an email here, and an email there, your subscribers have nothing to hang their coat on. They don't expect your emails, because when you're not there, someone else is. So their mind is not trained to expect you.

Think about this for a minute. The human mind relies on certainty. When it takes something for granted – and then that something is taken away, it feels naked, like there's something missing. Even if it's something that's not good for us. We crave familiarity. We crave certainty. We crave repetition.

Quicker Relationship Building

It's a lot more difficult to build relationships with people we only meet from time to time. When we are not there, others will take our place. This is why you need to be the constant. You will be the one they rely on for their daily dose on marketing advice. They can rely on you. It's hard to say that about the 3 day a week marketers.

Not everyone is going to love you just because you're emailing them every day. Some peeps just won't get you. That's completely fine. You must focus on building relationships with the people who do relate to you – and ignore everyone else.

Remember, you want to build a tribe of people who actually want to read your emails. Not a nation of people who scan through your emails and couldn't give a flying monkeys if you send a message or not.

The more you're there, the quicker people will get to know what you're about. Again, this is the repetition and familiarity thing here. You will build much quicker and much more solid relationships when you become the "one" marketer they can rely on.

Are you sending emails now? How often are you sending them? Do people contact you when you don't send an email message? I get emails all the time if I miss a day sending an email. It rarely happens that I miss a day, but it does happen – and when I do miss a day, I always get emails from people on my list asking where todays email is. This never happened to me when I was following the lemming rule of email message writing 3 days a week.

You Have More Content For Other Sources

Because I email my list every day. I always have content that I can share on other platforms. Most peeps will write a Flakebook post. Then write a separate blog post – and then a separate email message. This is madness and not a very wise approach to a business that should be heavily reliant on "Leverage"

Instead of scattering your attention from your blog, to your social media platform - and then onto your email marketing, you should be spending all that time writing great email messages that you then put onto your blog as a post – and then onto any other platform you're currently creating content for.

Not all your messages are going to be epic. But they don't have to be. You're writing every single day, so there's no pressure to get it perfect today, because you'll be there tomorrow too.

No other email marketer who writes 12 emails a month can say that. Besides, email marketing 3 times a week means you are under more pressure to get everything perfect today... because you won't be back writing for another couple of days. This leads me perfectly onto my last point which is...

You Make More Money Emailing Every day

I kept the best for last. The goal of an email list is to make money, right? So, how many promotions can you send to your email list if you're only emailing 3 times a week? Probably 1, maybe 2 – and that's pushing it because you are NOT providing enough value if your messages are more promotional than content rich.

The 3 times a week email marketer only has 1, maybe 2 shots at making a sale in any given week. And since the general consensus is that you should have more content rich emails than promotions... well... it obviously becomes increasingly difficult to make the sale. Why? Because peeps are not ready to buy when YOU want them to.

For whatever reason, you're going to miss people on any given day when you send out a promotion. You send your promotional email out on a Wednesday... but your subscriber gets paid on a Thursday. Whoops, just lost a sale. You send out a promotion on a Monday, but your subscriber doesn't get paid until Tuesday, or Friday, or whatever.

The point I'm making is that there could be a million different reasons why someone is not ready to buy your product on any given day – and since you only send one promotional email a week... you most certainly are going to leave a lot of money on the table. That's inevitable.

No matter what way you slice and dice it, emailing less often is going to lose you sales. Now, what if you're a daily email marketer. Well my sugar candy coated friend (no idea what that means) you have the advantage...

...the huge advantage of being there whenever your subscriber is ready to buy. And you have absolutely no reason to ever write a hard sell email message, because you are in no rush. You're there today, tomorrow, the next day...and the next after that.

Are you getting how powerful this really is. You can just write your daily entertaining emails that builds solid relationships with your subscribers... and place a link to your product at the bottom of every email. It will not be intrusive, but it will always be there. When someone is ready to buy... there you are. And where is the other 3 time a week marketer? nowhere to be found.

That doesn't mean you still can't hard sell inside your emails from time to time, but you'll find you won't need to force anything on your subscribers... because time is on your side.

When they're ready to buy... you're already there waiting... and they will become so accustomed to reading your messages, and so familiar with your personality, they will practically feel obligated to take your recommendation on board far quicker than anyone else who just drops in from time to time when they need money.

We all have friends we only hear from when they want money, right? Any other day they're nowhere to be seen, but when they want a few quid, they contact you. How does that make you feel? You feel cheated, right? They only get in touch when they want something off you. It's like you're being used, yes?

Think about that for a moment, because it's very important. If you're emailing every day. Building relationships every day.

Entertaining. Being interesting. Giving advice. Letting your subscribers into your world...

Do you think they will feel cheated when you ask for the sale? Nope. Quite the opposite in fact. You're always there. You don't just send them a message when you want to make money. You send a message every single day regardless of whether they buy from you or not. You essentially build much more trust as a result.

Compare that to the 3 day a week marketer. They only breeze into their subscribers inbox whenever they feel like it. They certainly are not, in most cases, a welcome guest – and yet, they ask for money. Hmmm... I know which marketer I would trust more.

Now, you still may have your reservations. I might not have convinced you that emailing every day is the best route to take. I can tell you one thing for damn sure though. If you ask any email marketer who sends daily messages to their list, whether they would be willing to cut down their message sending to 3 times a week, I know exactly what they would tell you.

Go ahead. Find a person who emails their list every day - and ask them would they change to 3 times a week. They won't. They won't because they already know the power of daily email messages – and they also know they will make a lot less money if they did so.

Try it the other way. Ask a person who only emails their list 3 times a week... to send daily emails. They'll tell you all the stupid reasons why it's a bad idea, but I guarantee the vast majority of people you ask, have never even sent daily emails – and yet they will tell you not to do it. It's these marketers that I can't stand. The ones who have never tried anything - and yet tell you not to do it.

That's my case for daily emails. Just because a marketer has a successful business – and emails their list 3 times a week, doesn't mean 3 emails a week is a good idea. They're succeeding in spite of their ignorance.

If they changed to daily emails... they would make a lot more money and build stronger connections with their subscribers. It's just common sense, but you have to do it right. You must inject your personality into your emails – and you must deliver your information in a way that engages your audience.

Just be yourself. Not every email has to be a training email. Be yourself. Be interesting. Be unique. Be controversial. Be YOU.

Conclusion To This Report:

I want to thank you so much for taking time out – and for taking a chance on this information. I sincerely wish you all the success in the world with your email marketing. We've covered a lot in this guide, but every piece of advice is worth putting into practice. Which is what you should be doing after you put this away.

- Think about setting up a reverse squeeze page to build initial trust "before" peeps get to read your free report.
- Use the structured template I laid out when creating your information products. When you get the hang of it, you'll be banging out cracking reports in no time. We need our readers to put our advice into action – and following my advice on creating information products

- makes that process a lot easier. Easier is good, right?
- Also use the email templates we discussed earlier when writing your messages – and add your own to the mix as you progress. The great thing about having templates to work off, is that it cuts down on the tedious task of creating the bloody content in the first place. It also has the added benefit of focusing your attention on the most important aspects of your task.
- Send daily emails. I realize this can be a big step for most, but the rewards are tremendously higher than being a "drop-in" to your subscribers inbox. Remember, we do crave familiarity – and we want, above all else, for our subscribers to feel like we're a part of their everyday marketing journey.

Thank you once again. It was a pleasure to write this report for you, but unless you take action with the content shared... it would have been a complete waste of both of our time. Take action, get stuck in, make it happen.

If you ever have any questions. Feel free to contact me at any time.